# Narcissists Exposed

# Narcissists Exposed

## 75 Things Narcissists Don't Want You to Know

### Drew Keys
Founder of Light's House.org

Light's House Publishing

Light's House books may be purchased for educational, business, or promotional use. For information, contact Light's House Publishing at www.lightshouse.org

First paperback edition published 2012.

ISBN-13: 978-1477483039
ISBN-10: 1477483039

Keys, Drew.
Narcissists Exposed: 75 Things Narcissists Don't Want You to Know / Drew Keys – 1$^{st}$ ed.

Light's House Publishing

This book is dedicated to
its readers, who are working
to prevent the narcissistic abuse of
themselves and their loved ones.

# Table of Contents

**Introduction**

**Chapter 1 – Identifying Narcissists**

Is narcissism bad?

Is narcissism a mental disorder?

What are the symptoms of NPD?

How many narcissists are there, and how can the estimates be accurate?

Can narcissists have more than one disorder?

Is narcissism treatable?

Can NPD be "cured"?

Does narcissism run in families?

How can I tell if someone is a narcissist?

How can I tell if I'm narcissistic?

What about an NPD "test" from the internet/a book?

Is my mother, my partner, a given political figure, or bad parent who is in the news lately a narcissist?

What's up with NPD and the DSM?


## Chapter 2 - What Are They Like

Are narcissists insecure?

Can a narcissist fall in love?

Are narcissists happy?

Are narcissists paranoid?

Do narcissists stalk?

What do narcissists like, love and want?

What do narcissists feel?

What would a narcissist say?

What do narcissists hate?

Can you help a narcissist?

Are narcissists dangerous?

What do narcissists fear/What hurts narcissists?

Where do narcissists work?

What do narcissists do to other people?

How do narcissists react to being ignored?


**Chapter 3 - Do Narcissists...**

Do narcissists know they're narcissists?

Do narcissists know what they're doing?

Do narcissists lie?

Do narcissists have friends?

Do narcissists love?

Do narcissists get worse with age?

Do narcissists do nice things for people?

How do narcissists end up?

Do narcissists have feelings?

## Chapter 4 - How They Operate

How do narcissists manipulate?

How do narcissists think?

How do narcissists choose the people they mistreat?

How do narcissists treat their children?

# Chapter 5 - Why Do Narcissists...

Why are narcissists mean / why do they lack empathy?

Why do narcissists lie?

Why do narcissists ignore you?

Why don't narcissists know they're wrong?

Why do narcissists want to hurt you?

Why do narcissists cheat?

Why do narcissists leave relationships?

Why (or when) do narcissists come back?

# Chapter 6 - Will a Narcissist Ever...

Will a narcissist ever apologize?

Will a narcissist ever change?

Will a narcissist come back/want you back?

Will a narcissist ever be happy?

Would a narcissist marry?

## Chapter 7 - When Narcissists...

When narcissists fail...

When narcissists attack...

When narcissists are nice...

When do narcissists cry?

When do narcissists devalue?

When a narcissist leaves?

When narcissists use children...

When your mother or father is a narcissist...

## Chapter 8 - Who Do Narcissists...

Who are narcissists nice to?

Who do narcissists target?

Who is attracted to (or marries) narcissists? Who do narcissists attract (or marry?) Who do narcissists love/fall in love with?

Who do narcissists cheat with?

## Chapter 9 - Handling Narcissists

Should you confront a narcissist?

How do you protect yourself from narcissists?

Should I feel sorry for a narcissist?

Should I ignore a narcissist?

If a narcissist ignores you...

Should you divorce a narcissist?

Should I tell the narcissist I know that they're a narcissist? What would they do?

How do you deal with narcissists/cope with them?

How do you make a narcissist feel guilty?

**Recovering From Narcissistic Abuse**

**Acknowledgments**

# Narcissists Exposed

## Introduction

Narcissists don't like it when people see through their tricks. It takes away their power. Intuitively, people who come into contact with narcissists seem to know this, and they feel that if they could ever just figure these self-absorbed manipulators out, the game would soon be over.

If you're reading this, you're probably one of those people who are trying to understand how narcissists operate, and you have plenty of unanswered questions about them. You're not alone; in fact, so do millions of other people. But as just one search of the internet will reveal, the answers to these questions aren't very quick or easy to find. This is unfortunate, because all that most people want to know is how narcissists typically behave in certain circumstances and why, and what they can likely expect from the narcissist *they* know. And they want it in plain English, as opposed to psychobabble.

The questions being asked on the net are constant, and they come from people who are feeling frustrated and confused. "Do narcissists know what they're doing, yes or no?" "Can someone tell me why the narcissist I know is suddenly ignoring me? What are they doing?" "I keep hearing conflicting things — just tell me what causes narcissism, really... " "What can I *do*?"

These kinds of questions are the ones I'm asked every day. I'm Light, owner of Light's House.org, a busy website for adult children of parents with personality disorders, and moderation team member at daughtersofnarcissisticmothers.com. I am an adult child of a narcissistic parent, and I began "no contact" with my narcissistic family in 2005. I've been immersed in the subject of narcissistic abuse and how to recover from it for many years. My work involves a lot of reading, writing, and answering questions about narcissism (and many other personality disorders).

By the beginning of my second year running Light's House, I'd begun noticing that the very same questions about narcissists were being asked of me repeatedly — questions like, "Do narcissists know they're narcissists?" "Why don't narcissists know they're wrong?" "Should we feel sorry for narcissists?" "How do you make a narcissist feel guilty?" "Are narcissists happy?" "Can narcissism be cured?" And many, many more.

Clearly, people aren't finding the answers they need.

There's no single resource dedicated to simply addressing the most common questions for people immediately and clearly. That's the gap I wrote this book to fill. What follows are the questions — and the answers — to the most popular questions (75, to be exact) that are asked of me over and over.

Before you read the questions, you should know that there are a few questions that science has not yet answered definitively, and that there are some questions that scientists seem to be changing their minds about with every new piece of ongoing research. This is the normal nature of research psychology, and when addressing the answers that have been changing the most, I have presented information based on the characteristic behavior of narcissists, which is solidly known and completely unchanging, and information based upon the shared universal experiences of narcissists' family members, who know them best. (Narcissists are not fond of therapy, and when compared to many of those with other disorders, they are poorly understood and defined, less often treated, and studied very little.)

This book is by no means an empirically-based project, and is not to be considered or used as a substitute for any type of professional advice. It is the passing along of the information I have gathered from the research and clinical information that is available, what I have personally learned firsthand as a result of my unfortunate and prolonged exposure to narcissists, and what I have read and discussed intensively with recovering adult children of narcissists on forums, blogs, websites, and in person.

The questions that follow are the actual top 75 questions asked of me, compiled from information based on visitor queries, feedback and search data sent to Light's House, from available research data, and finally, from the firsthand experiences of family members, partners, coworkers and friends of narcissists.

May you find the answers contained here informative and helpful.

Drew "Light" Keys
light@lightshouse.org

# Narcissists Exposed

# Chapter 1

## Identifying Narcissists

### Is narcissism bad?

A certain amount of narcissism (called healthy narcissism) is normal and not harmful to others. The desire to think about and value yourself and your own needs and wishes is healthy. However, certain more problematic narcissistic behaviors are considered indications of traits of Narcissistic Personality Disorder (NPD), and these are not considered mentally healthy. To view the complete traits list, as well as an explanation of how qualified clinicians use it for diagnosis, visit http://www.lightshouse.org/npd-the-disorder.html

## Is narcissism a mental disorder?

If a minimum number of certain requirements are met, a person can be diagnosed with Narcissistic Personality Disorder.

In the United States, NPD is listed in the Diagnostic and Statistical Manual that is used by psychologists, psychiatrists, and other mental health workers.

Narcissistic Personality Disorder is listed in the section of the DSM known as "Cluster B", which falls under a broader category, called "Axis II". NPD is described there, along with three (loosely similar) personality disorders. All four of the Cluster B disorders are listed below:

**NPD** - Narcissistic Personality Disorder (generally involving self-centeredness)

**BPD** - Borderline Personality Disorder (generally involving emotional instability)

**HPD** - Histrionic Personality Disorder (generally involving dramatic behavior — slated for removal from the DSM)

**AsPD -** Antisocial Personality Disorder (generally involving lack of conscience)

Mental health professionals refer to the Cluster B disorders as the "Dramatic and Erratic" personality disorders. All four of these disorders are known to create a high degree of interpersonal conflict, and can only be diagnosed by qualified clinicians.

If you are wondering if mere vanity by itself is a mental disorder, the answer is no. Vanity alone is not considered a mental disorder. It must be accompanied by at least 4 additional traits in order to be considered NPD.

Narcissism also ranges in severity. Some narcissists are more annoying and thoughtless than they are deliberately hurtful, and others (those with more malignant narcissism) are astonishingly cold and cruel.

## What are the symptoms of NPD?

At this writing, The American Psychiatric Association defines Narcissistic Personality Disorder as:

A pervasive pattern of grandiosity (in fantasy or behavior), need for admiration, and lack of empathy, beginning by early adulthood and present in a variety of contexts, as indicated by five (or more) of the following:

- Has a grandiose sense of self-importance

- Is preoccupied with fantasies of unlimited success, power, brilliance, beauty, or ideal love

- Believes s/he is "special" and unique and can only be understood by other special people

- Requires excessive admiration

- Strong sense of entitlement

- Takes advantage of others to achieve his or her own ends

- Lacks empathy

- Is often envious or believes others are envious of him/her

- Arrogant affect

This list is currently under revision and will undergo changes in 2013, so we will be seeing some modifications with regard to how Narcissistic

Personality Disorder is defined and diagnosed; however, NPD is slated to remain in the DSM.

## How many narcissists are there, and how can the estimates be accurate?

Research indicates the incidence of NPD is slightly less than 1% of the population (0.8)*. Researchers do not estimate the number of narcissists by studying narcissists. To arrive at this figure, *random members of the general population* are tested for traits.

*National Institute of Mental Health, Lenzenweger, et al (2007), Courbasson & Brunshaw.)

## Can narcissists have more than one disorder?

Yes. Anyone can have more than one disorder, and narcissists are no exception. People who have traits of one Cluster B disorder are also somewhat more likely to have traits from other Cluster B disorders. It's not all that uncommon to be dealing with a narcissist who also has traits from one or more of the other three Cluster B disorders (BPD, HPD or AsPD).

In addition, people with Narcissistic Personality Disorder do have a somewhat higher likelihood of having certain *other* mental disorders — such as mood disorders -- and a few others. Light's House keeps a complete list at the following address:

www.lightshouse.org/additional-disorders-narcissists-may-have.html

## Is narcissism treatable?

Several years of ongoing therapy is the recommended treatment for NPD; nevertheless, it is not considered a highly treatable disorder, and most narcissists refuse to genuinely commit to any kind of treatment at all, let alone agree they might ever have anything to improve upon.

## Can NPD be cured?

According to the available information, narcissists could moderately improve their behavior by employing a genuine desire to face what is wrong within the context of many years of skilled therapy;

however, this plan is something very few narcissists will ever implement. If anyone has told you that NPD is "curable", consider the source – are they trying to sell you a product? They probably are. If you ask this same question of a psychiatrist or psychologist whose practice includes regular contact with individuals who have NPD, you're not going to be given such hope, not by any means.

Most highly skilled clinicians will tell you to reduce or eliminate contact with a narcissist, because NPD makes people highly uncooperative and emotionally abusive.

Narcissistic Personality Disorder is highly resistant to change, and by and large, narcissists flatly refuse to make an honest effort at self-improvement the way most people will. And if you're wondering if you personally could ever make a true narcissist genuinely change, you should know sooner rather than later — you absolutely cannot.

## Does narcissism run in families?

Yes, although researchers have not yet figured out the entire picture with regard to why and how. A single study *(WJ Livesley, KL Jang, DN Jackson and PA Vernon)* has indicated a genetic predisposition to NPD.

## How can I tell if someone is narcissistic?

In addition to the above, there are many things you can look for. Not all narcissists do all these things, and some people who are not narcissists may do some of these things as well. These are just some key examples of noteworthy issues. Keep in mind that much of the following may be hidden, to prevent others from rejecting the narcissist:

- Lack of empathy and genuine concern for others

- Everything is "about them"

- Critical and judgmental behavior

- Wants to be obeyed, or pitied, or admired. Can become annoyed or angry when this does not happen

- Marked attachment to roles involving praise, credit, or power

- Usually serves others only because of underlying or hidden ulterior motives

- Fragile ego – cannot tolerate being questioned

- Disdainful, rejecting, resentful, snobbish

- Believes they are more physically attractive or more intelligent than others, often even if not

- Phoniness and lying to make themselves look better

- Inability to simply be one of the crowd, a beginner, or just play a small role — needs to immediately stand out as superior/special
- Misuse of power, can be highly disempowering of others

- Vindictiveness and smear campaigns against people who disagree with them or refuse to tolerate their manipulation

- Preoccupation (often hidden) with whether or not others form a favorable impression of them, as opposed to caring more about the quality of the relationship

## How can I tell if I'm narcissistic?

The short answer is, you could likely never determine this for yourself, and neither can any book. This is partly because narcissists don't admit to having such issues. If you were a narcissist, most likely, you'd simply give yourself a glowing evaluation.

But that's by far not the only reason why people can't self-diagnose, so only a proper clinical evaluation can determine if a person has NPD.

In addition, adult children of narcissists can have some issues and perceptions that may resemble behaviors that are characteristic of NPD due to their prolonged exposure to a narcissistic parent, and the complex task of determining the difference between any such potential issues and actual personality disorder traits is wisely left to trained professionals.

The following is a list of just a few issues to at least give some of your layperson's consideration to. If you believe these (or any other) personal issues may be concerns for you, seek the services of a properly qualified therapist who specializes in personality disorders:

- You've refused to go to therapy to honestly address things you need to work on - anyone with complaints is automatically just wrong about you

- You cannot easily see or freely admit that you have ever done things that are unkind

- *Non*-family members have suggested you have a big ego or are selfish/mean

- You don't allow people to question you without your getting upset, covering up or attacking them

- You think you're very smart/funny/talented, etc., but "enough" people don't seek your advice, laugh at your jokes, or think your magic tricks are all that great, and you think it's because something is wrong with them – they're stupid.

*A special note to adult children of narcissists: don't panic if you see any of the above in yourself. Just find yourself a good qualified therapist you like and make the changes you want.*

## What about an NPD "test" from the internet or a book?

Taking a self-administered personality quiz to see if you have NPD is a lot like taking a quiz to find out your level of physical attractiveness – by merely asking yourself whether *you* think you are good-looking. Your perception may be right, but it can just as easily be very wrong (*especially* if you're narcissistic).

Proper methods of testing NPD cannot be made publicly available. You must see a qualified diagnostician, such as a psychologist or psychiatrist, if you suspect an issue.

For many good reasons, everything else is not valid. If you are concerned you may have NPD, see a mental health practitioner who's got plenty of experience in dealing with clinical narcissism. They'll be refreshingly overjoyed to work with someone who will readily admit they're not perfect.

## Is my mother, my partner, such-and-such a political figure, or a bad parent who is in the news lately a narcissist?

Listen to *expert* opinions on the matter. Many of the best experts in the field have a doctoral degree from a university that has a good long-standing reputation. Some others are highly-experienced therapists who specialize in the treatment of personality disorders.

If you are wondering if someone well-known is a narcissist, make sure any information you read comes from a credible source. Even psychologists and psychiatrists cannot diagnose anyone they have not fully evaluated personally. The media is full of editorials, commentaries, and blog articles claiming a given celebrity or public figure is a narcissist. Unless a clinical diagnosis has been revealed, this is all just speculation.

Sometimes the label "narcissist" is put on people whom a certain segment of the public simply does not like. You can try to decide for yourself by looking for traits, but in the end, only a proper, in-person psychiatric evaluation could ever prove such a thing.

# What's up with Narcissistic Personality Disorder and the DSM?

The Diagnostic and Statistical Manual is the official guide that psychiatrists, psychologists, and many others in the medical and social service professions use to diagnose, understand, and treat mental disorders. NPD is listed under "Axis II" of the DSM, along with many other types of personality disorders.

At this writing, the DSM is under revision, which is done periodically to update the information it contains. You may have heard that NPD as a distinct personality disorder diagnosis might be removed from the DSM. This is no longer being considered.

The specific way in which Personality Disorders in general will be getting diagnosed is undergoing some change; however, NPD is now slated to remain in the DSM. For accurate ongoing information on the subject of the revision of the DSM, trust www.DSM5.org.

To directly reach the page addressing changes to the criteria and description of personality disorders, visit:

www.dsm5.org/ProposedRevision/Pages/
PersonalityDisorders.aspx

# Chapter 2

## What Are They Like?

### Are narcissists insecure?

Many have theorized that narcissists are narcissistic because deep down, they don't actually have good self-esteem; however, a 2006 study conducted at the University of Georgia, Athens, indicated the opposite – that the underlying self-esteem of narcissists is not low.* Narcissists do like themselves.

*Do narcissists dislike themselves "deep down inside"? W Keith Campbell, Jennifer K Bosson, Thomas W Goheen, Chad E Lakey, Michael H Kernis.

## Can a narcissist fall in love?

If you are defining "falling in love" as including genuine caring, you'll have difficulty trying to get "yes" for an answer on this one. There are quite a few people who've been involved with narcissists. They will tell you that when they first met the narcissist, they thought they'd found love, but in time, they completely changed their minds. The narcissist not only didn't seem to love them, but made them feel awful, used and abused, trashed, completely ignored, abandoned and betrayed, and even vehemently hated.

## Are narcissists happy?

This greatly depends on the definition of happiness used. Can a narcissist get up in the morning, check their appearance in the mirror to find that they still look good, catch up on their messages to find that everything is going their way so far today and sit down with their morning coffee and a big grin, knowing all is well in their self-centered world at the moment? Sure.

But can they really be deep-down happy when they're always feeling they have to be the biggest and best? Craving more attention, admiration or pity than others are interested in providing? Needing to have control all the time and escape emotional responsibility with lies? Always raging about the many things that cannot possibly go their way all the time? Most people would probably say it's highly unlikely, and that narcissism does not reflect real happiness, as much as narcissists want you to believe that they are always feeling amazingly fulfilled and on top of the world.

## Are narcissists paranoid?

A narcissist with no other disorders is not paranoid. A small percentage of narcissists do have Paranoid Personality Disorder as well as NPD, and those narcissists can be paranoid due to their PPD. Paranoid Personality Disorder is one of several disorders that narcissists are somewhat more likely than average to have, but most narcissists do not have PPD.

# Do narcissists stalk?

It's not impossible for some narcissists. There is no doubt that the typical stalker is mentally ill, and the causes of stalking are complex. If you are wondering if anyone you know is capable of stalking, it's best to first take immediate action to protect yourself and then contact a crisis center to explain your situation to a trained professional, who can help you.

I recommend the online resource, "Hot Peach Pages," which contains an astonishing amount of free information and contacts for those who have questions or need help. Hot Peach Pages is a global list of abuse hotlines, shelters, refuges, crisis centers, and women's organizations, plus domestic violence information in over 80 languages. Visit www.hotpeachpages.net and click on your country to begin.

# What do narcissists like, love and want?

Narcissists prefer control, and they like and love things that make them feel superior to and central to others. They want things that make them feel they are favored, in charge, greatly admired and respected, or more important than others. At times, and among different narcissists, these things may take any number of the following forms:

- Power
- Admiration
- Sympathy
- Attention
- Prestige
- Money
- Popularity
- Pity
- Control
- Influence
- Status
- Service
- Praise
- Obedience
- Possessions
- Recognition
- Entitlement
- Righteousness
- Good impressions
- Unquestioning loyalty

Narcissists' interest in these things isn't always obvious, however. They think that the above things are their birthright, so they are angry or upset when they do not get them, but merely satisfied when they do.

Most narcissists won't usually seem truly joyfully happy to have received any of the above things they want — just smugly satisfied or vindicated at best. This is because in their minds, the fulfillment of these wishes isn't a gift or a pleasure; it's the mere righting of a highly contemptible wrong. They believe it's how things should always have been, so it's about time that inferior service was fixed!

The above perception is part of why you can never please a narcissist. They're almost always miserable that the many things to which they believe they're so naturally entitled cannot actually be provided. This means they're often in a state of frustration and disappointment with others, condemning and controlling others to try making them provide the impossible.

# What do narcissists feel?

It's hard to say exactly how narcissists feel, because they're not honest, and non-narcissists can only observe and imagine. However, many of the same feelings non-narcissists have can also be observed in narcissists, although characteristically you won't see genuine empathy in narcissists.

Narcissists typically hide the feelings they think will cost them power, and will show you whatever feelings they think will help them gain influence over you.

# What would a narcissist say?

Narcissists say all kinds of things that reflect a lack of empathy for others. Things like, "Too bad", "What an idiot", "Whatever", and "I don't care" are said by most narcissists a lot, and even if they're not said, they're implied and thought.

Narcissists also say lots of things that put the blame on you or someone else. If you show any upset over your mistreatment, they will tell you that you're too sensitive and you overreact. You'll also be accused of not being able to "take a joke", and told that you're a cry-baby, or that you're actually "choosing" to feel hurt by something hurtful they did.

Narcissists who have hurt you typically use lots of excuses and gaslighting (denying they did what they did) and they may tell you that you're just jealous of them. They will invalidate you, telling you that you have a very "vivid imagination".

Some narcissists use pity and guilt to gain power, and these narcissists will say things to present themselves as martyrs, as weak ones who need your service, or as someone you have "wronged":

"I see you haven't called me again — your own mother, who sacrificed an award-winning acting career all for you!"

Because narcissists don't accept responsibility for things that make people feel bad, when questioned or told that something they did was inconsiderate, they commonly say things like, "I only did THAT because YOU did x... so it's actually YOU who caused this whole thing!" They may also tell you that they didn't mean it, or couldn't help it, when you know they must have, or they'll say that you've misunderstood their good, pure intentions. And your "misunderstanding" about them will always be because of your supposed shortcomings. Don't buy it.

## What do narcissists hate?

Narcissists hate:

- Being ignored
- Being questioned
- Being seen as common
- Being criticized
- Being disobeyed
- Being disregarded
- Having to respect other people's boundaries
- Being left out
- Coming second
- Being told they can't do or have something
- Having to follow the same rules as everyone else
- Not getting to be the boss

- Not being allowed special privileges
- Being asked to be more considerate
- Not getting their way
- Being disliked
- Not being well-served
- Not getting the attention they want
- Being told they're wrong or at fault in any way.

## Can you help a narcissist?

The short answer is no.

Ultimately, you can expect to get used and/or dumped for not infinitely trying to please them in every way possible.

In addition, if any person seems to need a lot of help from you, ask yourself why. Healthy people very rarely do.

## Are narcissists dangerous?

If someone you know makes you wonder whether they could be dangerous, then you should seek safety and contact professionals for skilled advice and assistance with your particular issue immediately.

If anybody makes you feel afraid or concerned that they may be capable of violence, regardless of what the reason may be, the smart thing to do is always to get away from them immediately and stay away.

Plenty of non-narcissistic people are dangerous, and you wouldn't wait to be told what their problems were about before seeking safety, so don't wait if someone you think is a narcissist is making you feel unsafe, either. Get away, stay away, and get protection first.

## What do narcissists fear, and what hurts narcissists?

Narcissists can likely be expected to fear things that represent losing power, influence and favor, since those are the things they desperately feel they must have.

However, the expression of narcissists' emotions don't often take the form of noticeable fear. Many narcissists appear to deny having fears. They will usually insist they're not afraid in the least, and they appear to be covering up more vulnerable emotions such as fear and sadness with emotions that suggest more threatening or unfazed responses, such as anger, denial, and indifference.

One exception to this pattern is seen in narcissists who use pity to manipulate. The expression of fear and other vulnerable emotions can help a narcissist gain control over your behavior. Such emotions can be used for the purposes of getting you to do what a narcissist wants, or to stop you from questioning them and/or asking them for consideration.

Narcissists know that when you feel sorry for them, they have a lot of power over you. It's very common for a narcissist who is being held accountable for mistreating others to suddenly turn the tables and play the martyr, the victim, or the innocent one who has been misunderstood.

Often, narcissists will not express hurt feelings as genuine sadness, but as denial, martyrdom, or narcissistic rage instead.

## Where do narcissists work?

Everywhere. Narcissists prefer power jobs in which they get to have the control, authority, attention, and credit, but not all narcissists are able to get and keep these jobs, so you'll find narcissists everywhere, from coffee shops to politicians' offices.

No matter the setting, however, the narcissist will be the one expressing general disdain for others, trying to be the boss, trying not to follow the rules, upsetting everyone else, lying, manipulating, and creating problems, and trying to gain attention, admiration or pity.

Certain professions do attract a higher-than-average percentage of people with NPD than other jobs do. Not surprisingly, these are the jobs that have lots of power and admiration attached to them.

Some examples of career fields that many narcissists find attractive are the medical field, the legal field, and the clergy. But while fields such as these do tend to have a higher than average percentage of narcissists in them, you can nevertheless still find at least one narcissist just about anywhere.

## What do narcissists do to other people?

Narcissists do lots of things that make other people feel bad. People with NPD are dishonest and phony, they make unkind comments, they twist things to suit themselves, they launch smear campaigns against people who stand up to them, and they demand that others do things their way.

Narcissists judge and criticize harshly, they deny they've done anything wrong, and they behave as if everything is about them. They're motivated primarily by their own interests, and they play power games and head games to manipulate and punish.

Narcissists play the victim, they control and ignore people, they take advantage, they throw tantrums, and they are highly vindictive and dishonest. Narcissists can be very hurtful.

## How do narcissists react to being ignored?

Narcissists hate to be ignored. They can be expected to get very upset about it if they feel overlooked, unheeded or treated as unimportant. Ignoring a narcissist can bring on narcissistic rage, which typically leads to any number of bad behaviors. Tantrums, manipulations, smearing, grandstanding, lying, playing victim, nasty retaliations, and refusing to cooperate are their most common reactions.

# Chapter 3

## Do Narcissists...?

### Do narcissists know they're narcissists?

A more useful way to phrase this might be, "Will most narcissists ADMIT they're narcissists?" The APA's definition of personality disorders does include limited insight into one's own behavior. However, recent studies indicate that narcissists do know they're narcissistic.*

Possible explanations for the fact that they might seem to be unaware of their narcissism likely involves not wanting to be held accountable and not wanting to be asked to change, or not wanting to accept the fact that others don't like what they see in the narcissist.

*Carlson, E. N. Honestly arrogant or simply misunderstood? Narcissists' awareness of their narcissism.

Carlson, E. N., Vazire, S., & Oltmanns, T. F. (2011). You probably think this paper's about you: Narcissists' perceptions of their personality and reputation. Journal of Personality and Social Psychology, 101, 185-201.

## Do narcissists know what they're doing?

Narcissists do know right from wrong, and unless they have another disorder involving impulse control, they do control their bad behavior when it suits them. For example, they may feel like raging at you or putting you down, but if someone they want to impress is nearby, they will usually save the personal attack for later.

It wouldn't be possible for them to do this if they had no awareness that what they were doing was unacceptable, so they are aware that the things they do are not okay; they just don't care enough about your feelings that they'll make an effort for your benefit — only for their own. This happens because narcissists cannot empathize properly.

More on this subject can be found at Light's House: http://www.lightshouse.org/do-narcissists-know-what-they-do.html

## Do narcissists lie?

Yes, narcissists lie a lot. They even lie to themselves, telling themselves they're wonderful and never do anything wrong. (The precise reasons why they do this have not yet been established). Narcissists are constantly seeking what's called "narcissistic supply", which can be very hard to access in an environment where the truth is not suppressed.

Narcissists lie when they insist they never said or did anything unkind or inconsiderate, they will lie to impress you, and they will lie to turn the tables in their favor, especially when they're enraged at someone who stands up to them.

Honesty is generally low on the list of a narcissist's priorities, especially when they are trying to prevent themselves from looking bad or appearing responsible for something that's problematic.

## Do narcissists have friends?

Yes, narcissists have friends, but not in quite the same way that non-narcissistic people have friends. Normal, healthy people are capable of having all kinds of friends, such as friends who have different values, friends who are assertive, friends who aren't perfect, friends with healthy boundaries, friends who may voice complaints, and friends who require healthy consideration. But narcissists don't have friends in that way.

Typically, narcissists will accept or "tolerate" certain people, as opposed to truly having friends, as long as these people don't step too far out of line with what the narcissist wants or ask more than the narcissist is willing to give. Most narcissists give very little (though they are usually hiding this fact so they won't be disfavored). A number of narcissists use giving to manipulate or gain favor with others.

In my work with those who are dealing with narcissists, I have found that people with traits of NPD generally have relationships with those who will easily slot into one or more of certain roles. With the exception of the term, "Flying Monkey", the labels offered below are my own; however, the roles themselves are as old as time.

## The Narcissist's Faux Friends

"The Underling" - this person knows less, or has less of something than the narcissist. People in this role make the narcissist feel much better about him or herself by comparison – just by being there for the narcissist to compare themselves favorably to. Underlings may be less intelligent, poorer, less attractive, or somehow otherwise "less than" the narcissist in the narcissist's mind.

"The Power Supply" - these are people who have some kind of advantage or access to something else the narcissist wants. The narcissist will charm, flatter and buddy-up to these people to gain secondary access to their prestige, power, benefits and influence. People in this role may hold a powerful position at work or in the community, they may simply be someone the narcissist wants to sleep with at the moment, or they may be someone who happens to have the power to deny the narcissist something that he or she is after.

"The Donkey" - this person does the undesirable work the narcissist won't do and doesn't want to pay a fair rate for. Typically, the narcissist figures out what they can easily spare that the donkey needs badly (either psychologically or materially). The narcissist then uses the donkey's desperation as leverage, making the donkey do their dirty work for little to no sacrifice on the part of the narcissist.

"The Duped Rescuer" - this is a person who thinks that the narcissist is just an innocent, powerless victim needing loyal, unquestioning protection and help. He or she believes the self-serving lies the narcissist tells about having been abused and will defend them without thoroughly considering the opinions of others or questioning the narcissist's accounts of his or her own behavior and experiences. If the duped rescuer has not known the narcissist long, they may realize that something is wrong in the coming months or years. If they have known the narcissist a long time, they're more likely to be in the role of a Flying Monkey (see below).

"The Flying Monkey" - someone who serves and defends the narcissist. This person (knowingly, or unknowingly) uses triangulation, social pressure, smear campaigns and any other means necessary to try controlling those who resist the narcissist. Flying monkeys may damage the reputation of those who reject the narcissist's power. This is "punishment" for behaving independently of the narcissist. The term flying monkey comes from the characters in the popular book series and film, "The Wizard of Oz".

"Coattail Friends" - these people want to have the power and influence the narcissist has, and seek friendship with the narcissist to associate themselves with the narcissist's power and influence. This is the same thing as the "Power Supply" friendship, above, except in reverse – the narcissist is sought out as someone's external source of power. Like most other friends of narcissists, coattail friends must continue to serve and/or please the narcissist if they want to remain attached to the narcissist's power.

# Do narcissists love?

Narcissists cannot empathize properly, and empathy is a cornerstone of the ability to love others. Particularly within the context of intimate relationships, narcissists are capable of wanting; however, whether what they feel can actually be classified as love is another matter.

Narcissism is something of a spectrum disorder. Those who are much more mildly affected seem to have slightly more ability to consider and appreciate people at times than more malignant narcissists, who can be utterly nasty much of the time.

While some current partners of narcissists may not be able to acknowledge their ongoing mistreatment, the majority of former partners of narcissists will tell you they did not feel loved and were not treated in a loving manner. This may be the best information to consider a possible answer to the question, since narcissists will insist that they do love you, even as they are repeatedly being hurtful, or even vicious. Many of those who have years of involvement with narcissists say that narcissists can't love – at least not in the way that non-narcissists do.

## Do narcissists get worse with age?

Narcissists intensely dislike getting older. Generally, they want to think of themselves as being forever perfect and unlimited – immortal. It's no surprise, then, that narcissists become more irritable and displeased as they age and begin to face the loss of ideal physical appearance and function. Narcissists do not make good dependents, or even good inter-dependents. They either bitterly and resentfully loathe the idea of needing the help of others or turn their increasing dependency into an unrelenting demand for pity, attention and unending servitude.

## Do narcissists do nice things for people?

Yes, most narcissists do nice things, at least on occasion. The majority of narcissists aren't 100% mean all the time. This is part of what makes things so confusing for the people they emotionally abuse. Decent behavior gives the abused person hope that the narcissist really does care, and could improve. Because after all, they figure, if the narcissist they know tips the paperboy, then somewhere deep down, they must actually care about others just like everyone does. But as many soon realize, narcissists actually don't.

Narcissists are also always on the hunt for opportunities to get "narcissistic supply", and a significant percentage of them play the hero to get it. So doing nice things for others is actually something some narcissists do constantly! They're doing such things for the credit and power that playing the role of the bigger, better, more saintly person gets them. Lots of these kinds of narcissists prefer work with children, the mentally or physically ill, in the clergy, with the elderly or mentally disabled, or with others who are less powerful and/or in need. There is tremendous opportunity for narcissistic supply in such helping positions, and plenty of power over people.

When considering someone's behavior, look very carefully not just at what they do, but for the underlying reasons why they do what they do. Are they really doing nice things because they share the other person's feelings and genuinely just want to help? Or are they more motivated by the power and esteem that comes with the role? When properly put to this test, narcissists fail.

## How do narcissists end up?

Some narcissists end up alone and friendless. Some end up surrounded by adoring codependent people who have never questioned them, and servants who still think the narcissist is completely innocent and wonderful. And they always will think this, even after the narcissist is gone, regardless of the hurt the narcissist has caused.

## Do narcissists have feelings?

Yes. Narcissists have feelings. Their ability to empathize is limited to non-existent, however. So, while they have plenty of feelings for themselves, it's difficult or even impossible for them to share in someone else's feelings the way others can. They may be pleased and proud if their pressured child does well at school, for instance, but they do not empathize well with what the child must be feeling.

Narcissists' feelings will always trump yours, and you will often be expected to ignore your own feelings in favor of theirs. They, however, will not do the same for you. They will be disinterested, distant, annoyed, angry, bored, or otherwise uninvolved in paying genuine attention to and valuing your feelings. A narcissist's feelings are always the most important thing to a narcissist, and he or she sees no reason why you should not think the same.

# Chapter 4

## How They Operate

### How do narcissists manipulate?

Narcissists want things their way, and nearly all their toxic behaviors are forms of, or can be traced back to, potential efforts to manipulate for control. Lying, ignoring, smear campaigns, playing the victim, false apologies, blaming, wheedling, and temper tantrums are used to get you to do the things they prefer. Narcissists will also "gaslight" (insist that negative events simply did not occur) leaving others to question their own memory and sanity.

Many female narcissists use social/family channels to wield the most power over others, playing the role of self-sacrificing martyr whose children are exceptional all because of her saintly efforts (or terrible, despite her tireless attempts to raise them so very well). Many male narcissists use work and achievement channels to wield the most power over others, and play the role of the golden king whose possessions are bigger, more attractive, and more easily attained by way of his supposed natural superiority.

There are certainly exceptions to this rule – all narcissists spend their time and attention wherever they feel maximum control can be attained. There are plenty of female narcissists whose greatest "power base" is at work, and male narcissists who bully coworkers and subordinates at work certainly do not check their NPD at the door when arriving home. But in the general sense, narcissism in women is loosely based more often on those things society says makes a woman powerful (appearance and family) and a man powerful (control and achievement).

## How do narcissists think?

Narcissists want to believe that they are something special, and they become very easily annoyed if you don't share that point of view. They want to believe that people regard them as exceptional – someone to revere and respect and give special rights and privileges to. When they come into contact with evidence that their fantasy is not shared by everyone else, they can become very angry or martyr-like and try to convince disagreeing people – in whatever ways they can, including dirty tricks and lying — that anyone who disagrees is absolutely wrong and should be somehow punished for the disagreement.

## How do narcissists choose the people they mistreat?

Narcissists don't necessarily choose people to mistreat so much as they just mistreat people on the whole. But some people, typically those who have experienced prolonged narcissistic abuse (and other abuse) as children, make very easy targets for narcissists. These people will be abused by narcissists more often and more severely.

Though it sometimes takes a little while, many people eventually see the narcissist for what they are and will avoid or reject them. This is how narcissists typically end up surrounded exclusively by dysfunctional people – healthy people turn away from them, and people who cannot identify and avoid their abuse stick around for more. In addition, narcissists often "discard" those who displease them.

By way of this 2-sided selection process, the narcissist can now maintain a circle of co-dependent people (often called co-narcissists) and other vulnerable people who will be punished or discarded if they fail to remain compliant with the narcissist's (sometimes hidden and denied) wishes.

The main exception to the general rule of many people coming to realize the narcissism present and rejecting it is in narcissists' families, where very few members will ever openly oppose narcissistic relatives, because this typically leads to sharp familial conflict and/or punitive rejection by most of, or all of, the family. This happens because, regardless of any superficial appearances to the contrary, narcissistic families are ultimately controlled by their narcissistic members.

People who have not yet healed from previous abuses succumb very easily to narcissists' tricks and will remain in contact far longer than most others. The most striking example of this is in narcissistic families, where most members never manage to evolve beyond the family's narcissistic patterns.

## How do narcissists treat their children?

Narcissists are terrible parents. They don't empathize with their children, so lots of things happen to children of narcissists that shouldn't. Some narcissistic parents are the "ignoring" type, and some are the "engulfing" type. (Some narcissistic parents do both). Ignorers are neglectful and disinterested in their kids, and their children are often targets for abuse by many. Engulfers are controlling and don't let their children breathe or grow up.

Some narcissists cannot stand any children, and some narcissists like only small children, because young children believe everything you tell them and are easy to manipulate and impress. Children of narcissists are virtually always given a dysfunctional family role, such as "golden child" (can do no wrong in the narcissist's eyes) or "scapegoat" (can do no right in the narcissist's eyes).

As parents, narcissists are emotionally abusive and toxic. Lying to their children, parentifying them, blaming them for things that aren't their fault and invalidating their feelings are the kinds of things narcissists do to their children. Much more detailed information about narcissistic parents is available at http://www.lightshouse.org

# Chapter 5

## Why Do Narcissists...?

### Why are narcissists mean, and why do they lack empathy?

Narcissists are mean because they don't have the proper amount of empathy for others. However, science hasn't yet proven why narcissists lack empathy. It may be brain-based; however, there is currently no scientific evidence of this possibility. As brain imaging technology advances, we will likely learn more.

### Why do narcissists lie?

Narcissists lie for all kinds of reasons. The most common reasons are:

- To impress
- To escape emotional responsibility
- To control and manipulate
- To save face
- To make people like them
- To get their way
- To convince themselves they're wonderful

Narcissists lie because they simply can't accept the inconveniences of a planet upon which most things cannot always go their way. They seek a fantasy world in which they are seen as above everything and everyone, and that's just not possible, so the lies are both a means of getting more of what they want and a way of remaining in a childish world of self-centered delusions. Opposing their lies will reveal narcissistic rage and martyrdom.

## Why do narcissists ignore you?

In the general sense, narcissists will ignore you because they have little interest in you unless you have something they want. However, when narcissists make an especially deliberate effort to ignore you, it is generally to increase their power and control over you.

If you do something a narcissist doesn't want, they will try to prevent you from doing it again, and they may do this by deliberately ignoring you. If you don't feed a narcissist's ego enough, if you question them, if they feel you're not paying enough attention to them, if they're angry at you for behaving too independently, if they just want an ego-fix, or if there's anything at all about you that makes the narcissist feel less powerful than they want to feel, they may opt to ignore you.

Such deliberate, concentrated ignoring is an attempt to make feel insecure so that you will apologize, come running closer to them, ask them what's wrong, and try to please them more. Narcissists prefer that you submit to their wishes and make their reality your primary concern. In a nutshell, narcissists ignore you when they want more power over you. They play the, "I'm more important, so let's just see how hard you'll work to try and get my attention now" game.

## Why don't narcissists know they're wrong?

Narcissists don't like others thinking they're wrong, and they will attempt to influence the opinions and choices of others by insisting they're right. Narcissists also just like to do things their way, and they know that the more vigorously they defend their way, the more often they will get it. Narcissists' desire for power over others can also take the form of devaluing the needs and wishes of others. This can be expressed as "I'm right... and you're not."

## Why do narcissists want to hurt you?

Because narcissists lack empathy and need to feel exceptional, they often do things that are hurtful, such as laughing at another person's difficulties, causing someone who's angered them to get into trouble, or putting people down.

Not every narcissist has the same degree and incidence of narcissistic tendencies, so one narcissist may seem much more deliberately hurtful than another. But all narcissists do hurt others quite often. They're very focused on, even obsessed with, their own worth and benefit, and they have little to no ability to empathize with others. It's not a good combination.

If you are dealing with someone who has narcissistic traits who also seems vicious, threatening, dangerous, lawless, unsafe or very cruel, you are probably looking at more than just NPD. You may find helpful information in materials pertaining to Antisocial Personality Disorder (sociopaths) and/or sadistic personalities. When dealing with anyone you feel is a threat to you, your very first priority needs to be your safety.

## Why do narcissists cheat?

This is another issue related to narcissists' insufficient empathy. If there's something a narcissist wants to do that could hurt the feelings of a partner, the narcissist will often go right ahead and do it anyway. Because a core component of pathological narcissism is inability to empathize properly, narcissists are not "tuned in" to the pain of others, even when they're the ones causing the pain. The impulse to cheat isn't going to be well controlled in a person who doesn't have much empathy for their partner's (or for another person's partner's) feelings, and this is why so many narcissists will cheat with tremendous ease.

Narcissists also believe they are entitled to do lots of things that mentally healthy people do not feel entitled to do. This contributes to their notoriously deplorable boundary violations as well.

## Why do narcissists leave relationships?

First, a narcissist may leave a relationship for all the same reasons other people do. Maybe they (or their partner) have changed, both people want a divorce, things aren't working out, etc. But the question behind the above question is likely, "Why do narcissists leave when others stay?"

Here's a list of some common reasons, all of which are, like the above items, are related to insufficient empathy:

- They're bored with their new "toy".
- You're not making a flat enough doormat – you're standing up for yourself.
- They meant to use you all along, and they're simply done now.
- They found a new dupe who doesn't yet realize that behind their shiny image is a creep.

- They're not thinking anything. They're just doing what they always do – whatever they want.
- They've decided you're "not good enough" for them.
- Your reasonable expectations are inconvenient.
- You haven't been worshiping them enough.
- They're punishing you for doing something they don't like, such as questioning them.
- Your request for consideration "victimized" them, and they need to "take care of themselves" now.

## Why (or when) do narcissists come back?

If ever it suits the narcissist to do so.

Narcissists will lie in order to make the person they're returning to think they are sincere. In reality, their new partner dumped them and they need a place to stay until they find somewhere else, the old partner simply turned out to be a better doormat/worshiper after all, or some similar reasoning that is based on their own wishes, and has little to do with feelings for the others involved. A narcissist will tell everyone otherwise, of course.

# Chapter 6

## Will a Narcissist Ever...?

### Will a narcissist ever apologize?

Not genuinely.

Most narcissists will respond to someone's legitimate concern with an excuse or anger. A narcissist's most popular excuse is that they only did what they did because of something someone else supposedly did wrong first, which then "made" them do it.

If narcissists feel they absolutely have to (to save their own skin, for instance) they will often issue what's called a "false apology". Typical false apologies include comments like, "I'm sorry you feel that way, but", "I'm sorry if you got hurt", and "I'm sorry, but if you hadn't done x..." -- or just a flat-out lie, saying they're sorry, when they're of course not feeling one bit sorry at all.

More about false apologies (and apologizing to narcissists) is available at Light's Blog: www.lightshouse.org/lights-blog.html/

## Will a narcissist ever change?

If a person has only mild narcissistic tendencies as opposed to NPD and/or attends skilled, long-term therapy, working earnestly and diligently, many clinicians will say there is hope.

However, this earnest willingness and long-term commitment is virtually non-existent in those with Narcissistic Personality Disorder, and the necessary process is by no means expected to be a short-term solution or a "cure" for NPD. This is because narcissists cannot admit that they are flawed in any way, and they typically abhor the concept of genuinely needing any kind of psychological help. (Some narcissists may go to therapy simply for regular narcissistic supply in the form of things like pity and attention. This is obviously not genuine therapy.)

When narcissists misuse therapy in this way, they want therapists whose skills, judgment and boundaries are very weak, so that the narcissist can proceed to manipulate them for narcissistic supply.

If this doesn't turn out to be the case and it becomes clear to the narcissist that the therapist actually has skill, good judgment and boundaries, and does expect the narcissist to make a genuine effort, their game is over. The narcissist's ploy usually ends after no more than just a few sessions at most, with the narcissist returning home and telling frustrated and disappointed family members, "Oh, that therapist said I'm fine; she said that there's nothing wrong with me and I don't need therapy..." I can't tell you how many times I've heard this very same lie reported by countless adult children of narcissists. In one narcissistic mother's outrageous version, she actually embellished the tale with, "...in fact, we sat and talked about HER problems, and I gave her some advice."

At this writing, the use of therapy on diagnosed Narcissistic Personality Disorder is considered to bring modest improvement after many years of skilled therapy.

## Will a narcissist come back/want you back?

Perhaps. But never for the right reasons.

They may return if their new partner doesn't turn out to be very submissive and overly-attentive after all, or if their old partner responded to their leaving by begging and pleading and becoming weak and desperately obedient, and they find that appealing. If this is the case, they may temporarily give the old partner some attention again in exchange for enjoying some of his or her increased submission.

Some narcissists like to play people against each other as well, and may have one or more person in the wings who are jealous and vulnerable enough that they'll desperately try to please the narcissist better to get them back or win them over against someone else. Narcissists prefer people who are desperate to please them.

## Will a narcissist ever be happy?

Narcissists want to believe that everyone will finally one day give them everything they want, and that can't ever happen, so in some sense, they'll probably always be angry and disappointed.

## Would a narcissist marry?

Yes, plenty of narcissists marry. It's not recommended that you be the spouse.

# Chapter 7

## When Narcissists...

### When narcissists fail...

When narcissists fail, they cover it up, deny it, lie, or do whatever else it takes to protect their image. Narcissists cannot easily accept that they fail. They may say things like, "Everyone makes mistakes" or "I'm not perfect" in order to try preventing someone from criticizing them, but those are just platitudes they're using as an ego shield. Narcissists can't truly admit that they really do make plenty of mistakes, and they want everyone to treat them as if they never do.

### When narcissists attack...

When narcissists go on the attack, they have likely experienced what is called a "narcissistic injury". (This is when a narcissist responds with narcissistic rage when a person makes them feel less than perfect or less than all-powerful and in control.) Avoiding contact with a narcissist who has gone on the attack is often helpful, as is making sure any contact that you DO have with them is in public, because they lie a lot when angry. Calmly appealing to someone reasonable who has more power than the narcissist can also be helpful.

## When narcissists are nice...

When narcissists are nice, they are virtually always doing it for something they want, or because it benefits THEM to do so. Don't make the mistake of thinking that someone who does nice things cannot be narcissistic. It's not at all true; in fact, a significant percentage of narcissists enjoy playing saint. In addition, even very toxic people can be nice, at least on occasion, especially if they do not feel threatened in the moment.

The simple performance of kind acts does not automatically render someone incapable of being significantly abusive.

## When do narcissists cry?

Narcissists cry for themselves. Because they lack empathy, when they cry, they are crying for what they personally wanted and didn't get, for the upset, loss or disappointment they feel, or to get your pity so you'll do more for them and give them more attention, more support, and more leniency.

A crying narcissist may be doing nothing more than manipulating you, and he or she may not even seem to realize that's what they're doing. In the general sense, when narcissists cry, they typically cry:

Real tears for themselves
Fake tears for power
No real tears for others


## When do narcissists devalue?

Narcissists devalue everything that is not in service to them, their values and their wishes. If it's not what they would do, have, be, think, etc., then it's not valuable. Narcissists also devalue people and deny that they're important to them, and more so if they've been questioned or opposed by those people.

Narcissists often practice something called "devaluing and discarding". This involves suddenly putting down, turning against, and rejecting someone who no longer pleases or serves them, immediately throwing the person away without a care. Because the discarded person has usually been believing most of the narcissist's lies that they are loved, the discarded person experiences a period of confused shock. The narcissist never really did love them after all, and suddenly, the mask is off — it's glaringly evident.

Mentally healthy people cannot vilify and throw a caring person away without a second thought. Devaluing and discarding is the virtually exclusive territory of those with Cluster B personality disorders such as NPD.

## When a narcissist leaves?

If a narcissist leaves you in the lurch, you are probably being "discarded". Narcissists do this when they are done getting as much as they can from you or when you start to ask them to be more considerate. (They hadn't planned on THAT, and it makes them angry!) You may feel awful when you are left, like you've been thrown away because you weren't "good enough", but that's a lie that narcissists try to make their discarded people believe. It's more likely you stood up for yourself, or were too strong for them in some way. Narcissists don't like people with strong, healthy boundaries or independent minds who may question them.

The real reasons narcissists throw people away are that they don't want to be bothered with things like being emotionally responsible, or they've found someone who defers to them more, or someone put a healthy boundary in place and asked for reasonable consideration, or they're just plain tired of someone and can't see the value in knowing them anymore.

Narcissists will discard you if you question them too much or fail to hide your feelings and needs consistently for their convenience and benefit. They don't want anyone's needs or feelings getting in the way of what they want. You have two choices when dealing with a narcissist in a relationship – be a doormat, or find yourself on the doormat.

Oftentimes there are head games to try getting you back under control first, and if you don't succumb, you'll then be discarded. These games include things like "Hoovering" (attempting to persuade you or even trick you into having unwanted contact with them) and indirectly using others to manipulate you.

## When narcissists use children...

Narcissists mistreat their children. Many of them do horrible emotional damage to their kids, and even more so during arguments, breakups and divorces. Because narcissists lack a normal amount of empathy, many of them will use their children as pawns without hesitation, attempting to manipulate their partner or ex-partner through their children. Adult children of narcissists overwhelmingly and unfailingly report that they wish somebody had done something about the mistreatment they received at home.

If you are the current or former partner of a narcissist, and your children are suffering, it is a good idea to seek the assistance of a child psychologist, who can give you some excellent tips and advice about how to love and support your children under such trying circumstances. In addition, should a custody dispute arise, if the psychologist has been working with your child, their testimony or letter of support can provide much-needed verification that your children have been emotionally abused by their other parent, and that you have been making every effort to attend to their psychological needs as a result.

## When your mother or father is a narcissist...

When your parent is a narcissist, you do not get your needs met as a child, and as an adult, you have a lot of work to do to get everything sorted. Learning to value yourself and your wants and needs is the single biggest issue that adult children of narcissists have to address. If you are the adult child of a narcissistic parent ("ACON"), you were either taught to put yourself dead-last or to play the role of entitled golden child, and healthy adults do not do either of those things.

Unraveling the sticky web in which you were raised takes lots of work. If you haven't gotten any therapy with a skilled therapist you like who has solid experience in working with personality disorders and children of people with personality disorders, get some; it is life-changing.

When looking for a therapist, do not select one and then decide that person will be your therapist no matter how you feel about them. That's the single biggest mistake ACONs make when choosing a therapist.

Any therapist you consider working with needs to have solid experience with NPD (ASK THEM ABOUT THIS!) and you should absolutely and positively like the therapist personally and feel good about how they treat you.

Selecting the right therapist usually involves several visits with at least a few. Be selective — a bad therapist can be far worse than no therapy at all.

More on this is available at: http://lightshouse.org/lights-blog/how-to-find-the-right-therapist

# Chapter 8

## Who Do Narcissists...?

### Who are narcissists nice to?

Narcissists can be nice to people who have something they want. Powerful people they want to be close to, people who can affect the narcissist's reputation for better or worse, and people who they want to do things for them will get treated very differently from others. This is one of the areas where the narcissist's two-faced nature appears most clearly. Narcissists can fly into a rage and mistreat somebody awfully just before the boss, teacher, rich acquaintance or influential public figure walks around the corner, and suddenly change their tune without missing a beat, smiling fakely, becoming charming and "thoughtful", friendly, concerned, and even jovial.

## Who do narcissists target?

Narcissists target for companionship and friendship those who are low in assertiveness, low in self-esteem, those who are less (or more) powerful than themselves, and those who can provide them with something or benefit them in some way.

Narcissists Target For Relationships:

Those with poor self-esteem and weak boundaries, those who readily put the needs of others above their own, those who have something the narcissist wants, those the narcissist thinks can help increase the narcissist's standing somehow, those who will serve them unquestioningly, and anyone else who provides them with what they want and doesn't question or confront them.

Narcissists Target For Revenge:

People who displease them. If you do not agree with a narcissist or you refuse to let them pull all the strings, they can become extremely angry. The more obviously or repeatedly you question or oppose them, the more likely you are to get badly smeared or otherwise mistreated.

## Who is attracted to (or marries) narcissists? Who do narcissists attract (or marry)? Who do narcissists love/fall in love with?

Sadly, the majority of people who are attracted to narcissists are those who were raised in a narcissistic home or environment, followed by anyone who was raised with emotional abuse of any type. Children of narcissists are shaped by the narcissistic family in which they were raised. Their self-esteem is low, they've been taught to defer all their needs, wants and wishes to someone else, and they're taught not to take any credit or make any requests, to expect very little, and to agree, even when they shouldn't. This is the perfect match for a narcissist!

The above behaviors are co-narcissistic behaviors. When a narcissist and a co-narcissist come into contact, unfortunately, their issues immediately slot together perfectly, like similarly-warped puzzle pieces. This happens on an unconscious (or barely conscious) level. Co-narcissistic people can be helped immensely with therapy that is provided by a therapist who specializes in issues related to personality disorders, and they would benefit from making every attempt to find one if they no longer want to end up with narcissists and other emotional abusers who lack empathy.

Co-narcissistic partners do not understand that any mistreatment they are receiving is not actually under their control, and they struggle endlessly to try "making" the narcissist care or change. (This is an unconscious attempt to resolve the childhood wounds they received at the hands of a narcissist or other abuser who could not love them.)

Often, narcissists will be more cooperative when a person behaves as they wish. This conditions the other person to be more compliant, apologetic and submissive when hoping to simply get their reasonable needs met by a narcissist.

The narcissistic partner fools their co-narcissistic partner into thinking that if only the partner could someday achieve the perfection the narcissist demands, the narcissist really would care more and finally treat the co-narcissistic partner with kindness and consideration. This is a lie that narcissists promote in order to keep their partners running around doing all the hard work and taking all the blame for everything. It works very well on co-narcissists and others who have co-dependent personalities.

People who have been narcissistically abused for extended periods are well-accustomed to the erroneous concept that if they are not absolutely perfect, then they have no rights at all. This is what narcissists "teach" their partners and children. Because no-one can ever be perfect, someone who demands perfection of others before being willing to give consideration to them is someone who actually has no intention of ever doing so.

But the lie that perfect compliance with a narcissist will finally bring thoughtful consideration is just that — a lie — and the co-narcissist always believes it, working harder and harder for a "reward" that does not actually exist. It's a trick designed to keep people giving and giving to the narcissist without the narcissist actually having to give anything back except more "charitable" lofty criticism about what's still not perfect. For narcissists, this game is their literal way of life.

## Who do narcissists cheat with?

Anyone they want to. A narcissist's cheating has nothing to do with you. They may try to fool you into thinking that the reason they are cheating with someone is your fault, because of things you do or don't do, or who you are/aren't. They do this because it makes you feel inferior and desperate to regain their attention, and they prefer that you be desperate and working hard to "improve" and earn their good graces. Often, they'll dangle what you want just out of reach and make you think it's attainable, but the reality is, it's all just a game to get what they really want – a feeling of control and/or superiority over you.

# Chapter 9

## Handling Narcissists

### Should you confront a narcissist?

If you want to confront a narcissist because you just have to get everything off your chest once and for all, and your only goal is to have your say without regard for the ugly consequences, it might be possible to get it said and feel satisfied despite the resulting nasty backlash (narcissists can be highly vindictive when confronted or rejected).

But if you want to confront a narcissist in the hopes that they will finally start to admit to the wrong things they're doing, or see anything your way, or finally genuinely apologize because they will start to really understand your pain, you're only going to be disappointed.

Above all, remember: you can't change a mental disorder with a confrontation. You can only change your own reaction to the disorder.

# How do you protect yourself from narcissists?

The best way to protect yourself from narcissists is to learn to identify them very early on in a relationship (or ideally, even sooner) and limit your contact with them as much as possible.

The following are some red flags to look for. Though not all narcissists do all of the things listed, and not everyone who may sometimes do something below is automatically a narcissist, steering clear of the following types of people can really make a big difference in terms of screening out narcissists.

- Avoid contact with people who:
- Are phony or dishonest
- Are judgmental and critical
- Are arrogant and self-centered

- Have to make sure you know all about their achievements/aspirations

- Like to give the impression that they're powerful and in control of others

- Strongly dislike children (especially older children) or;

- Especially like to impress or control young children

- Wouldn't ever dream of dressing unimpeccably -- nothing but the best will do

- Aren't genuinely interested in others, ignore you or others, have low curiosity about others

- Think that rules are for everyone else

- Like to make fun of others or engage in rude/insensitive putdowns

- Get upset when questioned

- Refer to other people and situations as "stupid" a lot

- Have children who seem astoundingly well-behaved, well-dressed, well-mannered and highly obedient; or --

- Have children who seem astoundingly badly-behaved, poorly-dressed, rude and highly rebellious.

- Are condescending, snobbish, cold, vindictive and bad-tempered.

- Think that when others are upset with them, it's just because they're "jealous" of them.

- Are prejudiced, and view any group of others as "beneath" themselves

- Don't like being asked to make reasonable changes on behalf of others

- Have control issues, especially issues pertaining to control of others

- Lie

- Are punitive

- Don't listen

- Seem two-faced

- Respond to feedback, questions and reasonable requests with defensive behavior/anger

- Never ask how you are and truly want to hear all about it

- Are impressed by or desire lots of status objects – luxury vehicles, ostentatious homes, etc.

- Talk about themselves most of the time

- Play the victim/Take up a lot of your time and energy with their complaints

- Aren't open to feedback about themselves

- Enjoy telling regular stories of ways they got the upper hand

- Demand the very best of everything, from toasters to health care providers

- Can never just be a participant – must always try to be seen as a leader

- Want everything their way

- Are full of excuses and blame others

- Think that their own personal experience represents all of reality ("how it IS")

- Weasel out of taking responsibility

- Overvalue personal impressions and social standing

- Play the saint and constantly seek to put themselves in admirable or powerful positions

- Never genuinely feel sorry or genuinely apologize

## Should I feel sorry for a narcissist?

There's no harm in feeling sorry for a narcissist. However, if by "feeling sorry for", you mean "be responsible for", or you think that feeling sorry for a narcissist means having to make yourself available to them for mistreating, then it's helpful to remember that you are actually only responsible for yourself and your children, which means not ever allowing you or them to be abused.

## Should I ignore a narcissist?

Narcissists hate being ignored, but sometimes it's the best plan. If a narcissist has targeted you in a smear campaign or similar, it's best to avoid them at all cost. A narcissist will be much unhappier (and more problematic) if they KNOW you're ignoring them, so it can also help if, as much as possible, you try to be subtle about the fact that you're doing so. If you're dealing with a narcissist in a work situation or other arrangement where you cannot get away, you can try avoiding them, which is somewhat more subtle than actual in-person ignoring.

## If a narcissist ignores you...

If a narcissist ignores you deliberately, they are likely doing it to gain control over you. Ignoring someone is a very powerful thing, because all people have a need to belong and to matter. Narcissists cash in on this need by ignoring people. They know that when some people are ignored, they will try harder to "win" the attention and caring they shouldn't have to work for. Co-dependent types apologize unnecessarily, try to make the narcissist happier and defer to the narcissist. They will do things that make the narcissist happy in the hopes of getting more sensitivity. This is the very dynamic the narcissist wants to continue.

If a narcissist is giving you the cold shoulder, they are most likely trying to reel you in closer so they can make you do what they want more easily. Adult children of narcissists and other emotionally abusive parents are especially vulnerable to this tactic. People raised in healthy homes do not respond to a cold shoulder by trying to please the person much more. Healthy people may make a comment about the matter or try to address it briefly, but they don't join in the game by trying to "make" the narcissist "like them better".

More functional people typically distance themselves in response to such a thing, ultimately. Manipulation tactics such as the ignoring game are most typically fallen for by people who were mistreated as children – until they heal.

## Should you divorce a narcissist?

If you are in a relationship with someone who has Narcissistic Personality Disorder, remember, you're not going to be able to make the narcissist truly change. Narcissists are emotionally abusive, and their relationships are unhealthy and based on whatever their own wishes are. There are many things to consider when determining whether it is right for you to maintain a relationship with someone. Those things aside, however, all narcissists mistreat their spouses and children.

The typical adult child of a narcissist suffers tremendously and greatly regrets that their other parent did not stand up for and protect them, and spouses are also very often badly mistreated.

Divorcing a narcissist can be much more complicated than initiating a typical divorce, especially with narcissists who are engulfing or who have been viewing the spouse as a symbol of their status or attractiveness. "Narcissistic injury" can also create lots of problems. In many cases where narcissists feel rejected by the spouse, they will rage and smear. (Some others will "devalue and discard", readily abandoning their entire family with astounding ease.)

For those divorcing narcissists, strong legal representation and excellent planning is recommended, as well as personal therapy for emotional and practical support.

## Should I tell the narcissist I know that they're a narcissist? What would they do?

People who have tried this find that it only backfires, because of the fact that essentially, narcissists cannot admit to their narcissism. The most typical responses received are:

Projection: "No, YOU'RE the narcissist here, that's exactly what YOU are!!"

Narcissistic rage: "How DARE you call me crazy after all I've done for you!"

Invalidation: "Puh-leeze! You're an idiot who has no idea what you're even talking about!"

Complete Disregard.

## How do you deal with narcissists/cope with them?

The ideal option is to avoid narcissists. Contact with a narcissist always involves mistreatment, and standing up to them only upsets or enrages them, causing them to smear and invalidate you, which makes the whole situation even more toxic and unbearable.

If you cannot easily avoid them, such as in work situations, try limiting your contact as much as possible. Don't waste a moment trying to make a narcissist treat you better. They simply will not. Don't take their abuse personally. They mistreat everyone who displeases them, and displeasing them is astonishingly easy to do.

## How do you make a narcissist feel guilty?

Narcissists don't seem to consciously feel guilty for their bad behavior, and this is why everyone wants to know if they can possibly make it happen somehow. You cannot truly make a narcissist express the kind of genuine apologetic sadness you might be wishing for. Narcissists are typically highly unempathic, and without a sense of empathy, such feelings of guilt are limited to non-existent.

True narcissism is a mental disorder that you personally will never be able to control. If you are asking yourself how to make a narcissist you know feel genuinely guilty for mistreating you, then you are caught in that narcissist's web, and getting yourself some skilled therapy is a very good idea.

# Recovering From Narcissistic Abuse

Most people who visit Light's House.org for information about narcissists are currently struggling with a narcissist they know. Because NPD is not significantly treatable, and because narcissists will not adjust their behaviors for the genuine benefit of anyone else, contact with a narcissist enables them to continue their abuse of you.

If you have been exposed to narcissistic abuse, whether as the family member of a narcissist, a significant other, a coworker, or a friend, your recovery path will be made easier by learning as much as you can about what you've experienced and why, and ultimately, by learning more about yourself and focusing on your own self-development.

The following are some common issues for those who have experienced abuse by narcissists:

- Low self-esteem
- Lack of assertiveness
- Fear of abuse of power
- Depression/anxiety
- Increased vulnerability to abuse
- Self-doubt
- Sense of unentitlement
- Toxic guilt and shame
- Self-invalidation

Narcissists gravitate toward people who have certain behavior patterns and weaknesses, and addressing the blind spots and issues that cause narcissists to prefer you in the first place is the key to preventing future narcissistic abuse. Until that's done, you'll continue to fall prey very easily to narcissists and others who lack empathy.

Where possible, it's a very good idea to seek assistance from a therapist who is specifically skilled in treating issues related to personality disorders. Where not possible, visit one of the many free online support forums. Links are listed on the Information & Support page at Light's House.

Additional information about narcissists is also available at the Light's House "All About Narcissists" index page: http://www.lightshouse.org/all-about-narcissists.html

If you have a question that is specific to your personal situation, I recommend speaking with a psychologist who specializes in personality disorders. If you have a general question about narcissism that was not addressed in this book or in the available content at Light's House, please send your question and the email address with which you purchased this book to: light@lightshouse.org within 30 days of your purchase for assistance.

The information contained in this publication is not to be used as a substitute for professional advice of any type.

# Acknowledgments

To my friends (both far and near) who have encouraged and supported me through all my challenges, including my work to overcome the effects of having had an ignoring narcissistic parent: MJ, Danu Morrigan, Dolly, P&O. And all the women at daughtersofnarcissisticmothers.com and visitors to Light's House. Each of you, in your own way, has helped me tremendously. Thank you.

Made in the USA
Monee, IL
14 October 2021